My Feelings

HAPPINESS

APP

Published by Creative Education
123 South Broad Street
Mankato, Minnesota 56001

Creative Education is an imprint of
THE CREATIVE COMPANY.

Design and production by EVANSDAY DESIGN

My Feelings

PINESS

LENORE FRANZEN

LIBRARY OF CONGRESS CATALOGING-IN-PUBLICATION DATA
Franzen, Lenore.
Happiness / by Lenore Franzen.
p. cm. — (My feelings)
Includes bibliographical references and index.
ISBN 1-58341-320-0
1. Happiness—Juvenile literature. I. Title.

BF575.H27F7 2004
152.4'2—dc22   2004049337

First Edition
9 8 7 6 5 4 3 2 1

PHOTOGRAPHS BY: Corbis (David Aubrey, Peter Beck, Manuel Blondeau/Photo & Co.,
Jonathan Cavendish, Patrik Giardino, Ted Horowitz, Ken Kaminesky, LWA-Sharie Kennedy,
Claudia Kunin, Roy Morsch, Reuters, Royalty-Free, Tom Stewart, Dana Tynan)

LINGS

Laughing 100 times is as healthy for you
as riding a bike for 15 minutes.

People feel many different things. They can feel mad, sad, afraid, or happy. These feelings are called **emotions**. Happiness is an emotion.

When you are happy, you feel good. You smile a lot. You want to be with other people. And they want to be with you. Happiness is easy to share.

When you feel happy, you feel like you can do almost anything. You may do better in school. You may make a new friend. You may run faster. People may call you a *ray of sunshine*. Or say you are *happy as a clam*.

ONS

H

WHAT MAKES YOU

A

PPY?

The smell of flowers or freshly baked cookies may make you smile.

You feel good when you eat healthy foods and get a lot of sleep. Exercise keeps your body strong and happy. When you are safe and warm, you feel happy.

You also feel good when someone loves you. Or when someone hugs you or gives you a **compliment**. A friend who shares with you can make you feel good, too.

Birthdays and holidays can fill you with joy. For some people, happiness is hearing a good story. For others, happiness is playing with a friend. Or getting a pet. Or learning to ride a bike.

Think about the last time you felt happy. What were you doing? You might feel good right now. Name the things that make you happy.

You use 15 different muscles
in your face when you laugh.

H

SHOWING YOU
ARE

HA

PPY

A round, yellow smiley face means *happy* to people around the world.

When you are happy, your whole body shows it. You may smile. Or clap your hands. You may skip or hop or dance.

Laughter is another way to show happiness. You laugh with your face **muscles** and your voice. Some people say, "Laughter is the best medicine." Laughter makes you feel better. It helps your body fight **disease**.

You may have a special way of showing happiness. You may wink or snap your fingers. You may squeeze someone's hand. You may even shout or act silly.

musc

When you see something funny,
your brain sends a message to
your face to laugh.

Y

OU

R JOY

A dog wags its tail when it is happy.
A happy cat purrs.

When you feel good, you should share your happiness with other people. You can cheer up a sad friend by drawing him a picture. You can tell your grandma a funny story or give her a hug. You can pick flowers for your neighbor. Or play a game with your little brother or sister.

Happiness is like having a lot of something good. Do not waste it! Be a friend to someone. Share a toy. Say something nice to someone. Smile. When you share your joy with others, it grows and grows.

GOOD TALK

When you make someone feel good, you feel good, too!

What You Need

FIVE OR MORE PEOPLE

PAPER

A PENCIL

A BOWL

What You Do

1. Have each person write his or her name on a piece of paper.

2. Put the names in the bowl.

3. Take turns drawing a name from the bowl. Say something nice about that person (for example, she runs fast; he is funny; she plays piano well).

4. Have each person describe how it feels when someone says something nice. What feels better, saying something nice or hearing it?

WORDS TO KNOW

compliment a nice thing someone says about another person

disease sickness; something that makes you ill

emotions feelings; sadness and fear are kinds of emotions

joy another word for happiness

muscles parts of the body that help you move

READ MORE
EXPLORE THE WEB

Porter, Eleanor H. *Pollyanna*. New York: Dover Publications, 2003.

Rylant, Cynthia. *The Cookie-Store Cat*. New York: Blue Sky Press, 1999.

Wilhelm, Hans. *All for the Best!* Charlotte, Va.: Hampton Roads Publishing Company, 2003.

Wyeth, Sharon Dennis. *Something Beautiful*. New York: Doubleday Books for Young Readers, 1998.

KIDSHEALTH: WHY YOU SHOULD SMILE
http://www.kidshealth.org/kid/feeling/emotion/smile.html

PAM PETTY'S CREATIVITY WEBPAGE
http://www.pampetty.com/creativity.htm

INDEX

2.7/.5